First
Facts®

# Investigating CONTINENTS

# SOUTH AMERICA

## A 4D Book

by Christine Juarez

PEBBLE
a capstone imprint

**Download the Capstone  app!**

- Ask an adult to download the Capstone 4D app.
- Scan the cover and stars inside the book for additional content.

When you scan a spread, you'll find
fun extra stuff to go with this book!
You can also find these things
on the web at www.capstone4D.com
using the password: samerica.31824

First Facts are published by Pebble,
1710 Roe Crest Drive, North Mankato, Minnesota 56003
www.mycapstone.com

**Library of Congress Cataloging-in-Publication Data**
Names: Juarez, Christine, 1976–
Title: South America : a 4D book / by Christine Juarez.
Description: North Mankato, Minn. : Pebble, 2019. | Series: Investigating continents
Identifiers: LCCN 2018004114 (print) | LCCN 2018010878 (ebook) | ISBN 9781543531848 (eBook PDF) |
ISBN 9781543531824 (hardcover) | ISBN 9781543531831 (pbk.)
Subjects: LCSH: South America—Juvenile literature.
Classification: LCC F2208.5 (ebook) | LCC F2208.5 .J83 2019 (print) | DDC 980—dc23
LC record available at https://lccn.loc.gov/2018004114

**Editorial Credits**
Cynthia Della-Rovere and Clare Webber, designers; Svetlana Zhurkin, media researcher;
Kathy McColley, production specialist

**Photo Credits**
Capstone Global Library Ltd, 5, 9; Shutterstock: Christian Vinces, 17, DFLC Prints, 8, Don Mammoser, 15,
Filipe Frazao, cover (top), Galyna Andrushko, 11 (inset), Hans Wagemaker, 14, Iurii Kazakov, 13, Lenorko
(pattern), cover (left) and throughout, MMPOP, 11 (back), Nicole Derick, 21, RPBaiao, 9 (inset), San Hoyano,
7, tateyama, 19, Thiago Leite, cover (middle), Vadim Petrakov, cover (bottom left), Viacheslav Rashevskyi,
cover (bottom right), back cover, 1, 3

Printed and bound in the USA.     PA017

# Table of Contents

# About South America

There are seven **continents** on Earth. South America is the fourth biggest continent. It is mostly surrounded by water. To the west is the Pacific Ocean. To the east is the Atlantic Ocean. A narrow strip of land joins South America to North America.

PACIFIC OCEAN

**continent**—one of Earth's seven large land masses

# CONTINENTS OF THE WORLD

ARCTIC OCEAN

NORTH AMERICA

EUROPE

ASIA

ATLANTIC OCEAN

AFRICA

EQUATOR

INDIAN OCEAN

SOUTH AMERICA

AUSTRALIA

SOUTHERN OCEAN

ANTARCTICA

# Famous Places

In South America there are many famous places. Machu Picchu is an **ancient** city high in the Andes Mountains in Peru. It was built more than 500 years ago.

A famous **modern** structure is in Brazil. It is a huge statue of Jesus Christ. It stands on top of a mountain. The statue was built between 1922 and 1931.

Machu Picchu

**ancient**—from a long time ago
**modern**—up-to-date or new in style

# Geography

South America has different land types. The world's largest mountain range is on the west coast. It is called the Andes. It stretches for about 4,505 miles (7,250 kilometers).

A large part of South America is covered by **tropical** rain forests. The largest rain forest is the Amazon. It is home to the Amazon River.

**Fact:** The highest point in South America is Mount Aconcagua in Argentina. It is 22,831 feet (6,959 meters) tall.

**tropical**—hot and wet

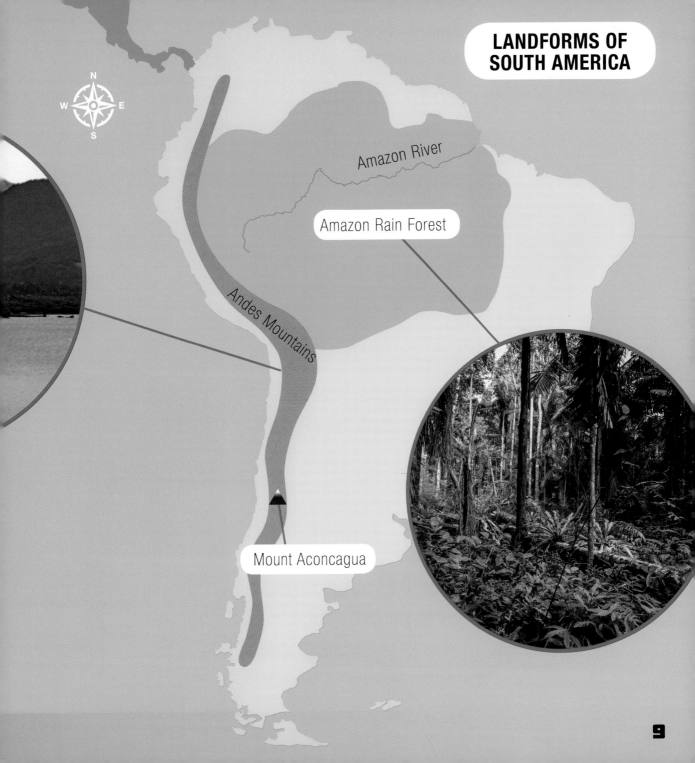

# LANDFORMS OF SOUTH AMERICA

Amazon River

Amazon Rain Forest

Andes Mountains

Mount Aconcagua

South America has many large bodies of water. The mighty Amazon River is the longest river in South America. It is the second longest river on Earth.

Large lakes are found in South America. Lake Titicaca is high up in the Andes Mountains. Tall reeds grow around the edges of the lake. Local people use the reeds to make huts and fishing boats.

**Fact:** The Amazon River is 4,000 miles (6,437 km) long. That is one and a half times the width of the United States.

Lake Titicaca

Amazon River

# Weather

South America has many different types of weather. The grasslands are hot and dry. It is even drier in the deserts. The Atacama Desert is one of the driest places on Earth. It is hot and wet in the rain forests. High in the mountains, it is very cold. It is also cold and windy at the southern tip of South America.

Rain never falls in parts of the Atacama Desert in Chile.

# Animals

All kinds of animals are found in South America. Andean condors soar above the mountains. Large **rodents** called capybaras live in forests and grasslands.

The Amazon rain forest is home to thousands of types of animals. Wild cats called jaguars live there. There are also birds, lizards, monkeys, frogs, and insects.

jaguar

**rodent**—a mammal with long front teeth used for gnawing; rats, mice, and squirrels are rodents

Andean condor

# Plants

South America's rain forests are thick with tall trees and many plants. Long vines twist around tree trunks.

One type of South American plant is rare. Known as the queen of the Andes, it grows in the Andes Mountains. It only flowers once in its life. This is when it is between 80 and 150 years old. After it flowers, the plant dies.

Queen of the Andes is also called puya raimondii.

# People

About 425 million people live in South America. The continent has 13 countries. Sáo Paulo in Brazil and Buenos Aires in Argentina are the continent's biggest cities.

Most people in South America speak Spanish. In Brazil, people speak Portuguese. Ancient **native** languages are also spoken in South America.

Buenos Aires, Argentina

**native**—something or someone naturally found in a country without being brought to it

# Natural Resources and Products

South America has many **natural resources**. Valuable products come from rain forests, such as wood, nuts, and palm oil. Oil comes from Venezuela. Colombia has coal and also produces precious emeralds. The grasslands of Argentina are used for farming. Farmers grow crops and keep cattle and sheep. These farms are some of the biggest in the world.

cattle in Argentina

**natural resource**—a material from nature that is useful to people

# Glossary

**ancient** (AYN-shunt)—from a long time ago

**continent** (KAHN-tuh-nuhnt)—one of Earth's seven large land masses

**modern** (MOD-urn)—up-to-date or new in style

**native** (NAY-tuhv)—something or someone naturally found in a country without being brought to it

**natural resource** (NACH-ur-uhl REE-sorss)—a material from nature that is useful to people

**rodent** (ROHD-uhnt)—a mammal with long front teeth used for gnawing; capybaras, rats, mice, and squirrels are rodents

**tropical** (TRAH-pi-kuhl)—hot and wet; places near the equator are tropical

# Read More

**Kalman, Bobbie.** *Let's Learn about Earth's Continents.* My World. New York: Crabtree Publishing, 2018.

**Leavitt, Amie Jane.** *The Animals of South America.* A Continent of Creatures. Kennett Square, Pa.: Purple Toad Publishing, 2017.

# Internet Sites

Use FactHound to find Internet sites related to this book.

Visit *www.facthound.com*

Just type in 9781543531824 and go.

 Check out projects, games and lots more at
**www.capstonekids.com**

# Critical Thinking Questions

1. What is the largest rain forest in South America?
2. Why do you think South America has so many different kinds of weather?
3. South America is home to the Andes Mountains, the Amazon River and surrounding rain forest, and the ancient city of Machu Picchu. Which of these would you most like to visit? Why?

# Index